Stories for Illustration

For Mason

Stories for Illustration

Diana Kimpton

First published in April 2014

Diana Kimpton
25 Solent View Road, Cowes
Isle of Wight PO31 8JY

www.dianakimpton.co.uk

Cover picture from istockphoto.com

ISBN 978-09573414-4-9

Contents

About this Book

The five stories in this book are all picture book texts waiting for someone to illustrate them. Three of the stories have been published as full colour picture books that are now out-of-print while the other two are brand new.

If you are an aspiring illustrator, you can use these stories to practise your skills. You are welcome to use any of them in work for college or for your portfolio, but please credit me as the author.

If you are a parent or teacher, you can use these stories to stimulate your children's imaginations and encourage them to create their own illustrations in their heads or on paper.

If you want to use the stories with your class, you have my permission to copy the text for use on a whiteboard or on worksheets, but please credit me as the author.

There are only two restrictions on use.

1. You mustn't sell copies of any of the stories, with or without illustrations.

2. You mustn't put the entire text of any of the stories online, with or without illustrations.

However, I'm happy for you to put a few illustrated pages online to show other people what you've created. If you do that, I would appreciate a link to this book to show the source of the story.

How to Illustrate a Picture Book

These are the stages used by professional illustrators. You don't have to follow them if you don't want to, but you may find them helpful.

First decide which story you are going to illustrate and read it carefully, looking for important issues to consider when you draw the pictures. You'll find some illustration tips at the end of each story to help you.

Now draw some sketches of your main character from different angles to make sure you have made the right choice. At this point, you can also decide which media you will use for the illustrations. The different types of paint can produce a variety of effects, and some illustrators combine them with ink or coloured pencils to add extra detail.

The next step is to decide how you are going to divide the text between the pages. I've put gaps in the stories to help you think about this, but you can ignore them if you wish. What's important is to make sure that the page turns come in the best possible places. Sometimes you can make them reveal a secret or a surprise.

A traditionally published picture book has 32 pages, but some of those are taken up with the title page and copyright page. If you want to practise illustrating this type of book, you'll need to restrict yourself to 12-14 double page spreads plus a single page at the beginning and maybe one at the end. It often works well to finish the story on the last spread and just have an extra picture on the single page at the end.

You are now ready to create what are called roughs. To do this, decide which pictures will appear on each page and draw a line drawing of each one. Don't forget to leave space on the page for the text.

Change and tweak the roughs until they fit the story well and look good. You might want to let someone else look at them at this stage as they may spot mistakes that you have missed.

When you are happy with the roughs, you can start to create the full colour pictures that will appear in the final book. This stage is called the final artwork and, when it's finished, you can put the text and pictures together to create your book.

Writing the text directly onto your pictures risks ruining your hard work if you make a mistake. It's safer to put the words on transparent overlays or to scan the pictures onto your computer and use editing software to add the text. These two methods also let you experiment with different fonts and layouts without damaging the final artwork.

The Bear Santa Claus Forgot

First published by Scholastic in 1994 with illustrations by Anna Kiernan

Christmas Eve was nearly over. Santa Claus yawned. Just one more visit to make and then he could go home.

The sleigh landed gently on Madeleine's roof. Santa Claus put the last few toys into a sack and swung it onto his back.

But the sack was old. It had a hole in one corner.

"Eek," said the bear, as he slid through the hole.

"Ouch," said the bear, as he landed with a bump on the floor of the sleigh.

He sat up and rubbed his head. He could see Santa climbing down Madeleine's chimney without him. That wasn't right.

He was Madeleine's bear. The label round his neck said so. She had asked Santa for him weeks ago. What would she say in the morning when he wasn't there?

When Santa came back, he didn't notice the teddy bear sitting all by himself. He just climbed onto the sleigh and whistled to his reindeer. They galloped away, pulling the sleigh up into the night sky.

First the sleigh turned to the right.

"Oops," said the bear, as he tumbled across the floor.

"Ouch," said the bear, as he bumped into the side of the sleigh.

Then the sleigh turned to the left.

"Oops," said the bear, as he tumbled across he floor.

"Ouch," said the bear, as he bumped into the other side of the sleigh.

Next the front of the sleigh pointed up into the air, as the reindeer galloped higher and higher.

"Oops," said the bear, as he tumbled across the floor.

"Help," cried the bear, as he bounced out of the back of the sleigh.

The bear grabbed desperately for something to save him. As the sleigh flew off, the teddy bear dangled from the back by his front paws.

"Phew," said the bear, as he held on very tight. His paws ached, but at least he was safe.

Then he looked down and saw the roof of Madeleine's house far below him. "That's where I should be," he thought. "If Santa won't take me, I'll have to go by myself."

The bear shut his eyes and let go.

"Aaargh," said the bear, as he fell through the air.

"Eek," said the bear, as he spun round and round with his arms and legs outstretched.

"Ouch," said the bear, as he landed with a thump on Madeleine's roof.

He sat up and blew some snow off the end of his nose. The snow was cold and damp. It made his hair go spiky.

The bear scrambled up a pile of snow and looked down the chimney.

Inside it was dark and scary. He didn't want to go down there, but how else could he get into Madeleine's house?

"Oooh," said the bear, as he climbed nervously into the chimney pot.

"Aaargh," cried the bear, as he slid down the chimney.

"Ouch," said the bear, as he landed in the fireplace with a cloud of soot and ash.

There was no Christmas stocking by the fireplace.

There was no Christmas stocking under the tree.

"It must be beside Madeleine's bed," thought the bear so he started to climb the stairs.

The stairs were very tall for a bear. The stairs were very steep for a bear.

"Phew," said the bear when he got to the top. He wanted to stop for a rest, but he couldn't. He had to hurry. It was nearly morning.

He walked along the landing and peeked around the first door.

"Hmmm," said the bear with a shake of his head. He could hear a dripping tap. He could smell soap.

This wasn't Madeleine's room.

He peeked around the second door.

"Hmmm," said the bear with a shake of his head. He could see a big bed with two people in it. He could hear snoring.

This wasn't Madeleine's room.

He peeked around the third door. "Ah ha," said the bear. He could see a little girl fast asleep. He could see a Christmas stocking hanging on the end of her bed.

This must be Madeleine's room.

But the stocking was very high for a bear.

"Oh," said the bear, with a tear in his eye. There was no way he could get into

Madeleine's stocking. There was no way he could be a proper Christmas present, unless...

"Hmm," said the bear, as he scratched his head thoughtfully. In the corner of the room were some leftover Christmas decorations.

"Ho ho," said the bear, as he rolled himself up in a sheet of wrapping paper.

"Eek," said the bear, as he fell flat on his back.

"Aah," said the bear, as he looked up at the stocking.

He was badly wrapped up, a little bit damp and rather sooty, but he was in just the right place - well, nearly, anyway.

That's where Madeleine found him in the morning, and she loved him straight away.

Illustration tips

It's very difficult to draw a teddy bear climbing stairs. Anna avoided the problem by drawing a picture of him at the bottom of the stairs and another of him at the top, without any pictures of him part way up. You might like to do the same.

Remember that, once he's fallen down the chimney, the bear needs to look sooty all the way to the end of the story.

A Good Place for Kittens

First published by Scholastic in 1998 with illustrations by Kathryn Prewett

It was windy and raining. The cat was worried. She had been searching all day without success and she was running out of time. Before it was dark, she must find a good place for kittens.

She strode across the short grass.

She swished through the long grass.

She found an old wooden box and looked inside.

Perhaps this was the right place.

But the cold wind blew through the gaps between the wood.

This wasn't a warm place.

This wasn't a good place for kittens.

The cat squeezed between the railings.

She tiptoed through the mud.

She found a hole under a tree and looked inside.

It was warm.

Perhaps this was the right place.

But the rain dripped into the hole.

This wasn't a dry place.

This wasn't a good place for kittens.

The cat prowled between the puddles.

She padded past the wall.

She found an empty oil drum and looked inside.

It was warm.

It was dry.

Perhaps this was the right place.

But the bottom of the drum was hard and scratchy.

This wasn't a comfortable place.

This wasn't a good place for kittens.

The cat wriggled underneath the fence.

She scrunched down the gravel path.

She found a garage and looked inside. It was warm.

It was dry.

It was comfortable.

Perhaps this was the right place.

But a dog came and growled at her.

This wasn't a friendly place.

This wasn't a good place for kittens.

She fled across the garden.

She plodded down the road.

She found a house, but the door was shut. She couldn't look inside.

The cat felt very sad. It was nearly dark, and she was too tired to go on searching.

She looked at the house again. There was a window open, but it was very high up. It would be hard to reach, but she had to try.

She scritch-scratched up the tree.

She wobbled along the branch.

She leapt onto the window sill and through the window.

Inside the house, it was warm.

It was dry.

It was comfortable.

It was friendly.

It was exactly what she wanted.

She lay in front of the fire and purred. This was a good place for kittens. And, in the night, this was the place where her kittens were born.

Illustration tips

The page turns are extra important with this story as it works best if the reader has to turn the page to find out what's wrong with each place the cat finds.

Remember to make the weather dark and stormy all the way through and to make sure the cat looks fat enough to be pregnant.

If you include the tree in your picture of the cat looking at the house, you'll give children the chance to spot how she can get inside.

Doctor Hoof

*First published by Scholastic in 2011
with illustrations by Garry Parsons*

When Doctor Hoof moved to Willows Ford, he nailed a notice to his new front door. It said

DOCTOR HOOF
HORSE DOCTOR
I ONLY TREAT HORSES

Then he sat back and waited for his patients to arrive. He waited and waited. But nobody came. Willows Ford was a one-horse town, and that one horse was Doctor Hoof.

By the end of the week, Doctor Hoof felt very lonely.

"This isn't the right place for me," he decided. "I'd better move somewhere else."

He was just starting to pack when there was a knock at the door.

"I'm Basil Bray," whispered the donkey. "And my throat is very sore."

Doctor Hoof shook his head. "I can't help you. I only treat horses."

"But donkeys aren't very different," said Basil "Look! I've got hooves just like you."

Doctor Hoof realised Basil was right. So he gave him some medicine to make him feel better.

Doing that made Doctor Hoof feel better too. So he changed the notice on his front door to say

DOCTOR HOOF
HORSE DOCTOR
I ONLY TREAT HORSES
AND DONKEYS

A little while later, there was another knock on the door.

"I'm Walter Woof," said the dog. "I've got a thorn in my foot."

Doctor Hoof shook his head. "I can't help you. I only treat horses and donkeys."

"But dogs aren't very different," said Walter. "Look! I've got four legs and a tail, just like you."

Doctor Hoof realised Chester was right. So he pulled the thorn out of the dog's paw to make him feel better.

Doing that made Doctor Hoof feel better too. So he changed the notice on his front door again.

DOCTOR HOOF
HORSE DOCTOR
I ONLY TREAT HORSES
AND DONKEYS AND DOGS

Doctor Hoof went inside again. Almost immediately, there was another knock on the door.

"I'm Henrietta Hop," said the mother rabbit. "My son, Harry, has cut his ear."

Doctor Hoof shook his head. "I'm a horse doctor. I only treat horses and donkeys and dogs. But I'm sure you're going to tell me that rabbits aren't very different."

"Of course I'm not," said Mrs Hop. "Rabbits aren't like horses at all."

"My ear hurts," said Harry, and he started to cry.

Doctor Hoof felt sad as he watched the tears pour down Harry's face. "Maybe rabbits aren't very different to horses. My ear would hurt too if I cut it."

He put some ointment and a bandage on Harry's ear to make him feel better.

Doing that made Doctor Hoof feel better too. So did the carrot Mrs Hop gave him for being kind. He went to the front door and changed his sign again.

DOCTOR HOOF

HORSE DOCTOR

I TREAT HORSES

AND DONKEYS AND DOGS

AND RABBITS

Doctor Hoof crunched his carrot thoughtfully as he read what he had written. Then he had a brilliant idea. He picked up his pencil again, crossed out the last line and changed his sign one last time.

DOCTOR HOOF

HORSE DOCTOR

~~I TREAT HORSES~~

~~AND DONKEYS AND DOGS~~

~~AND RABBITS~~

I TREAT EVERYBODY

From then on, Doctor Hoof had lots of patients and lots of friends. And he never thought of moving again.

Illustration tips

Horses don't naturally stand on their hind legs or hold things with their hooves so you'll need to draw a cartoon horse rather than a realistic one.

If it's easy to read the words on the notice in your picture, you may want to leave them out of the text.

The Night Mare

Not previously published

"I don't want to go to sleep," Emma told Grandma. "That's when the bad dreams come – the ones with the scary ghosts and the enormous monsters and the big, fierce tiger."

"Bad dreams are just nightmares," said Grandma, as she gave Emma a bedtime kiss. "You don't have to let them frighten you."

Emma lay in bed, all alone, and tried to stay awake. She wished Grandma was right. But she didn't know how to stop being scared.

Suddenly she heard a noise outside. She peeked through the window and saw a beautiful horse standing in mid-air.

"I am the Night Mare," whinnied the horse. "Come ride with me."

Emma scrambled onto the Night Mare's back. Then she grabbed hold of the mane with both hands and said, "Let's go!"

The Night Mare galloped up into the sky. She soared through the clouds and dived down into a different world.

"Oh no!" cried Emma as the horse's hooves touched the ground. This was the forest she always dreamed about – the one where all the scary things lived.

The ghosts slid out from between the trees, wooing and hooing.

Emma cringed away, hardly daring to look. But the Night Mare stamped one front foot and stared hard at the ghosts. "Go away!" she ordered.

To Emma's surprise, the ghosts did as they were told. They sank into the ground and disappeared.

The Night Mare trotted on, carrying Emma further into the dream forest.

Tramp! Tramp! Tramp! The monsters marched out of the wood, rumbling and grumbling.

Emma cringed away. But the Night Mare stamped her other front foot and stared at the monsters. "Go away!" she ordered.

To Emma's delight, the monsters did as they were told. They shivered and shrank until they were no bigger than mice. Then they fled back into the forest, squeaking and wailing.

The Night Mare trotted on, carrying Emma deeper into the dream forest. Emma tightened her grip on the Night Mare's mane. She knew what was coming next.

The big, fierce tiger sprang onto the path in front of her. It waved a huge paw and roared.

Emma felt its hot breath and saw its sharp teeth. But this time she wasn't scared. She was sure the tiger would go away when the Night Mare told it to.

But the Night Mare didn't say anything to the tiger. Instead, she turned her head towards Emma and said, "It's your turn now. You know what to do."

Emma slid down from the Night Mare's back. She stood in front of the tiger, put her hands on her hips and stamped her feet. "Go away, bad tiger," she ordered. "I'm tired of you spoiling all my dreams."

The tiger looked very surprised. He closed his mouth, put his tail between his legs and ran off at top speed.

From then on, Emma never had bad dreams again – well, hardly ever anyway. And when she did, she knew exactly what to do. She told all the scary things to go away. Then she whistled for the Night Mare and flew on her back to a happier dream.

Illustration Tips

The challenge with this story is to draw ghosts, monsters and a tiger that are scary enough to make Emma's reaction reasonable without being so frightening that they terrify your readers.

The Night Mare can fly, but it's up to you whether she has wings or not.

Counting Memories

Not previously published

"Will Dad come soon?" said Jason.

"Just as soon as he can," said Gran. "While you're waiting, let's have a look in my box of memories."

The memory box was made of shiny brown wood. Jason opened it carefully and took out:

1 doll with a china face

"She's almost eighty years old," said Gran. "My mum was given her when she was a little girl. And my mum was your great-grandmother."

2 toy soldiers

"The paint's come off," said Jason.

"That's because they're very old.

They belonged to your great-grandad when he was only as big as you are now. He grew up to be my dad."

3 shiny medals

"They were your great-grandad's too. He got them for being brave when he was a soldier, but he never liked to talk about it very much."

4 baby's bootees

"My mum knitted these for me when I was a baby," said Gran. "Look how tiny my feet used to be."

5 Russian dolls

"When I was a little girl, my uncle was a sailor. He travelled all over the world and brought these back for me.

6 records

"I loved these songs when I was a teenager. My dad used to shout at me for playing them too loud."

7 charms on a golden bracelet

"Grandad gave me that just after we were married. It was to remind me of everything we'd done together.

8 ducks on elastic

"Your dad loved those when he was a baby. They fastened across his pram, and he used to laugh all the time when he played with them."

9 stripes on a teddy bear's jumper

"That's Henry – your dad's best bear. He lost him once when he was a little boy and had to go to the police station to get him back."

10 jewels on a cardboard crown

"Look, Gran. It fits me," said Jason.

"And you look just like your dad did when he wore it in the school play."

11 toy footballers

"They were your dad's too," said Gran. "Grandad used to take him to football matches when he was small."

"Dad takes me now," said Jason.

12 numbers on a clock

"Your dad made that at school. He was so proud when he bought it home to show us."

13 shells from the beach

"One summer, we went to the seaside for a holiday. Your dad was much better than me at finding shells."

14 paints in a box

"Your dad used to use those," said Gran. "He was always good at art."

"So am I," said Jason.

15 silver horseshoes

"They were on your mum and dad's wedding cake. Your mum looked so beautiful that day and they both looked so happy."

"Was I there?"

"No. You weren't born yet."

16 foreign coins

"Grandad and I brought these back from the holiday we had in Spain with your mum and dad."

"Was I there?"

"Not quite."

17 silk flowers

"Grandad gave me these on the day that

you were born. You were our first grandchild, and we were so excited when we saw you for the first time."

18 glittering glass beads

"When you were a baby, you loved to play with my necklace and one day you pulled it so hard that it broke."

"I'm sorry," said Jason.

"Don't worry," said Gran as she gave him a hug. "I wasn't even a little bit cross. I've only kept the beads to remind me what a happy baby you were."

19 stars on a picture

"I remember this," said Jason. "I made it for your birthday."

"And I've kept it to remind me of you," said Gran.

Just then, Dad ran in. "You've got a new baby sister," he said, as he picked Jason up and swung him around. "And Mum's sent a card especially for you."

The card said "Happy New Sister Day" and inside were …

20 kisses

Jason was delighted. "We can put it in the memory box."

"That's a lovely idea," said Gran. "Then we'll never forget our happy time together waiting for your sister to be born."

Illustration Tips

This counting story is designed to introduce young children to the sequence of family history. There are lots of different ways to illustrate it.

Are you going to show the counting objects in a separate part of the page or in the main picture? Are you going to show the history of the objects? Are you going to show Gran and Jason looking at the objects?

There is no right way to answer those questions. You can use any approach you like and maybe try different approaches on different pages.

Remember that Mum needs to look pregnant in the picture for 16 foreign coins to help readers understand Gran's comment.

About Diana Kimpton

I have written more than 40 books for children, including my Pony-Mad Princess series, other novels, picture books and non-fiction. I have always loved horses and find that writing about them gives me the perfect excuse to spend time at the stables when I should be working. But I don't just write pony books. My work covers a wide range of topics, and I love the challenge of researching something new.

In 2012, I was so excited by the changes in the world of books that I started publishing my own work. I'm so glad I did, because it's fun and it's given me the freedom to produce this rather unusual book. I hope you've enjoyed it and found it useful.

When I'm not writing books or playing with horses, I enjoy creating and running websites in partnership with my husband, Steve.

You can find me online by visiting

- my author website at
  www.dianakimpton.co.uk

- my blog at
  www.horsesanddragons.co.uk

- my site about writing and
  self-publishing at
  www.helpwithpublishing.com

You can also find me on Twitter where my username is @dianakimpton

Some of Diana's Books

There Must Be Horses

A novel about a foster child who wants a home with horses.

For ages 9+, teen and young adult

Princess Ellie to the Rescue

and twelve other titles in the Pony-Mad Princess series. For ages 6+

The Secret Necklace

and seven other titles in the Amy Wild - Animal Talker series. For ages 6+

The Lambaroo

A picture book about a lamb adopted by a kangaroo. For ages 3+

Perfectly Pony

A mixture of pony facts and pony stories based on real events. For ages 7+